Heinemann

active maths

Pupil Book 3
Multiplication and Division

Authors: Peter Gorrie, Lynda Keith, Lynne McClure, Amy Sinclair

How to use this book

Contents

Instructions look like this. Always read these carefully before starting.

These are Rocket activities. Ask your teacher if you need to do these questions.

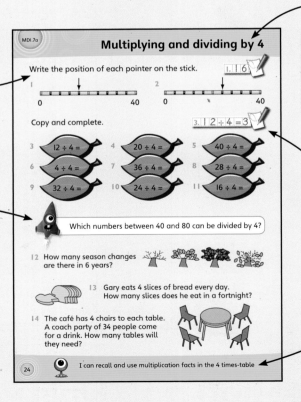

Each page has a title telling you what it is about.

This shows you how to set out your work.

Read this to check you understand what you have been learning on the page.

Multiplying

How many beakers on each tablecloth?

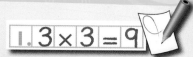

Draw a grid to match each multiplication. Write the number of squares.

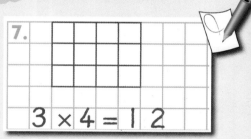

7. 3 × 4 = 1 2

7. 3 × 4

8. 2 × 5

9. 4 × 5

10. 6 × 2

11. 5 × 5

12. 3 × 10

13. 2 × 2

14. 9 × 2

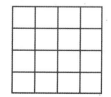

Write multiplications to match different square grids, e.g. 4 × 4 = 16.

I can make multiplication sentences to match arrays

3

Multiplying

How many stickers on each sheet?

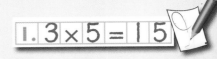

1. $3 \times 5 = 15$

1

2

3

4

5

6

7

8

9

Draw and label two grids that match each number.

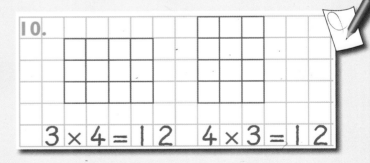
10. $3 \times 4 = 12$ $4 \times 3 = 12$

10   12

11   20

12   15

13   6

How many grids can you draw that have 24 squares?

I can make multiplication sentences to describe arrays

Multiplying

Write pairs that show the
same multiplication.

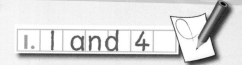

1. 1 and 4

2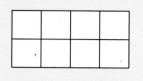

3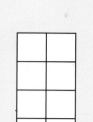

4

1

5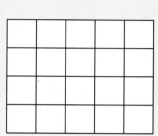

6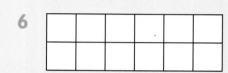

7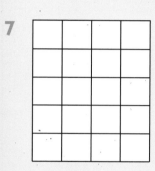

8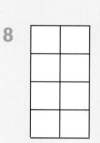

9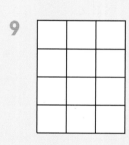

10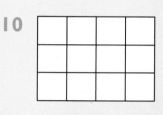

Use 12 squares to draw as many rectangles as you can.

Make another multiplication using
these numbers and find the answer:

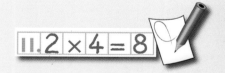

11. 2 × 4 = 8

11 4 × 2   12 3 × 5   13 8 × 2

14 4 × 6   15 7 × 3   16 2 × 9

17 6 × 3   18 5 × 4   19 6 × 7

I can compare arrays and know which ones are the same

5

Multiplying

Write two multiplications
for each set of pegs.

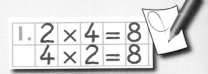

1.
| 2 × 4 = 8 |
| 4 × 2 = 8 |

1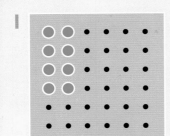

2

3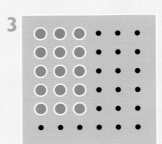

4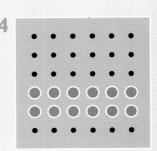

5

6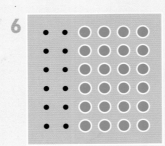

7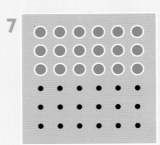

8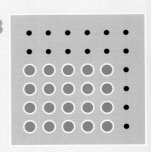

Copy and complete.

9 3 × 3 = ☐

10 4 × 2 = ☐

11 5 × 5 = ☐

12 5 × 2 = ☐

13 3 × 5 = ☐

14 4 × 3 = ☐

How many different
multiplications can
you show on a 6 × 6
pegboard? Use between
10 and 20 pegs. Draw
them on squared paper.

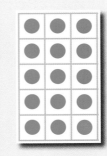

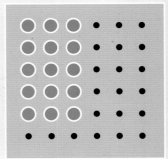

I can make up multiplication sentences to describe arrays

Multiplying and dividing

Write a division for each set.

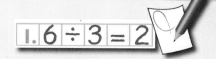

1. $6 \div 3 = 2$

 **1**  **2**  **3**  **4**

Write a matching multiplication for each set.

Draw pictures for these divisions.

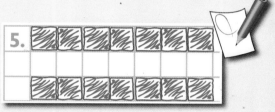

5.

5	$14 \div 2$	6	$9 \div 3$	7	$15 \div 5$	8	$20 \div 4$
9	$10 \div 2$	10	$24 \div 6$	11	$30 \div 10$	12	$25 \div 5$

Write a multiplication
and division for each set.

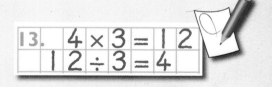

13. $4 \times 3 = 12$
$12 \div 3 = 4$

13  **14**

15   **16**

 I can write multiplication and division sentences to describe a picture

Multiplying by 2

Write the position of the pointer on each stick.

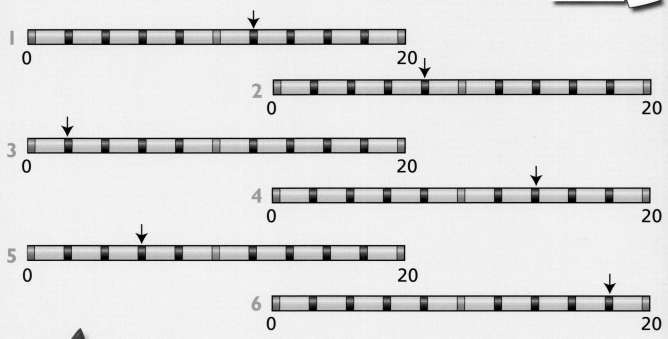

Draw your own counting stick from 0 to 20.
Mark four places on the stick. Write the positions.

Copy and complete.

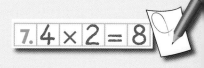

7   4 × 2 = ☐   8   7 × 2 = ☐   9   ☐ × 2 = 10

10 3 × 2 = ☐   11 8 × 2 = ☐   12 ☐ × 2 = 18

13 5 × 2 = ☐   14 10 × 2 = ☐   15 6 × 2 = ☐

16 ☐ × 2 = 6   17 ☐ × 2 = 4   18 9 × 2 = ☐

I can build up the 2 times-table

Fours

Copy and complete the grid.

1	2	3	4
5	6		

Write the last number in the:

1 2nd row

2 10th row

3 5th row

4 4th row

5 3rd row

6 7th row

7 6th row

8 9th row

Each animal has four legs. Write the number of legs in each set of animals.

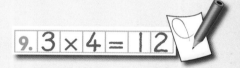

9. $3 \times 4 = 12$

9

10

11

12

13
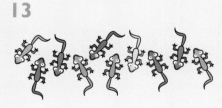

14

Think of things in your life that you count in 4s.

I can build up the 4 times-table

Fours

Copy and complete using doubling.

1   3 × 2 = 6

2   5 × 2 = 10

3   7 × 2 = ☐

4   4 × 2 = ☐

5   9 × 2 = ☐

6   6 × 2 = ☐

7   8 × 2 = ☐

3 × 4 = ☐

5 × 4 = ☐

7 × 4 = ☐

4 × 4 = ☐

9 × 4 = ☐

6 × 4 = ☐

8 × 4 = ☐

Make the 8 times-table using the 4 times-table.

Each chair has four legs.
Write the number of legs.

8

9

10   2 × 4 =

11   3 × 4 =

12   10 × 4 =

13   7 × 4 =

14   4 × 4 =

15   9 × 4 =

16   6 × 4 =

17   5 × 4 =

18   8 × 4 =

 I can build up the 4 times-table by doubling the 2 times-table

Eights

Each boat in the race has eight rowers.
Write the number of rowers in each group.

1

2

3

4 6 boats

5 8 boats

6 7 boats

Write how many boats are needed for these rowers:

7
16 rowers

8
48 rowers

9
56 rowers

10 24 rowers

11 32 rowers

12 80 rowers

If each boat can only take six rowers, how many boats
are needed each time? Are there any spaces left?

 I can build up the 8 times-table

Tens

Each bus has 10 passengers.
Write the number of passengers.

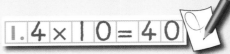

1

2

3

4 6 buses

5 8 buses

6 7 buses

Write how many buses are needed for these passengers:

7 20

8 50

9 80

10 30

11 70

12 100

If each bus can only take eight passengers, how many buses are needed each time? Are there any spaces left?

I can build up the 10 times-table

Fives and tens

Write a multiplication
for each set of toes.

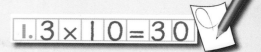

1. $3 \times 10 = 30$

1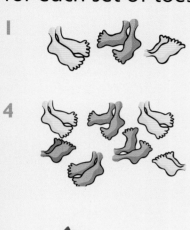

2

3

4

5

6

7

 How many toes in your classroom? Include your teacher.

Write a multiplication
for each set of fingers.

8. $5 \times 5 = 25$

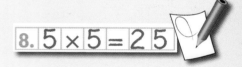

8

9

10

11

12

13

14

15

16

 I can build up the 5 and 10 times-tables

Fives and tens

Write the value of each pile of coins.

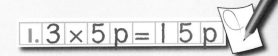

1. $3 \times 5p = 15p$

1

2

3

4

5

6

7

8

Write what must be added to make each pile worth £1.

Write the position of the pointer on each stick.

9. 15

9
0   50

10
0   50

11
0   50

12
0   50

13
0   50

14
0   50

15
0   50

16
0   50

I can build up the 5 and 10 times-tables

Fives and tens

Write the cost.

1. $4 \times 5p = 20p$

Soak the Teacher

5p a throw

I 4 throws	2 2 throws	3 7 throws
4 10 throws	5 20 throws	6 6 throws

Find how many throws you can have for each coin: 1p, 2p, 5p, 10p, 50p, £1, £2…

Copy and complete.

7. $4 \times 5 = 20$

7 $4 \times 5 = \boxed{}$ 8 $6 \times 10 = \boxed{}$ 9 $7 \times 5 = \boxed{}$ 10 $4 \times 10 = \boxed{}$

11 $6 \times 5 = \boxed{}$ 12 $8 \times 5 = \boxed{}$ 13 $7 \times 10 = \boxed{}$ 14 $9 \times 10 = \boxed{}$

A clever way for multiplying by 5 is:

multiply by 10, then halve it

For example: $9 \times 5 \longrightarrow$ $9 \times 10 = 90$
half of $90 = 45$

Use a clever way to try these:

15 $7 \times 5 =$ 16 $12 \times 5 =$ 17 $21 \times 5 =$

18 $32 \times 5 =$ 19 $46 \times 5 =$ 20 $14 \times 5 =$

 I can build up the 5 and 10 times-tables

Threes

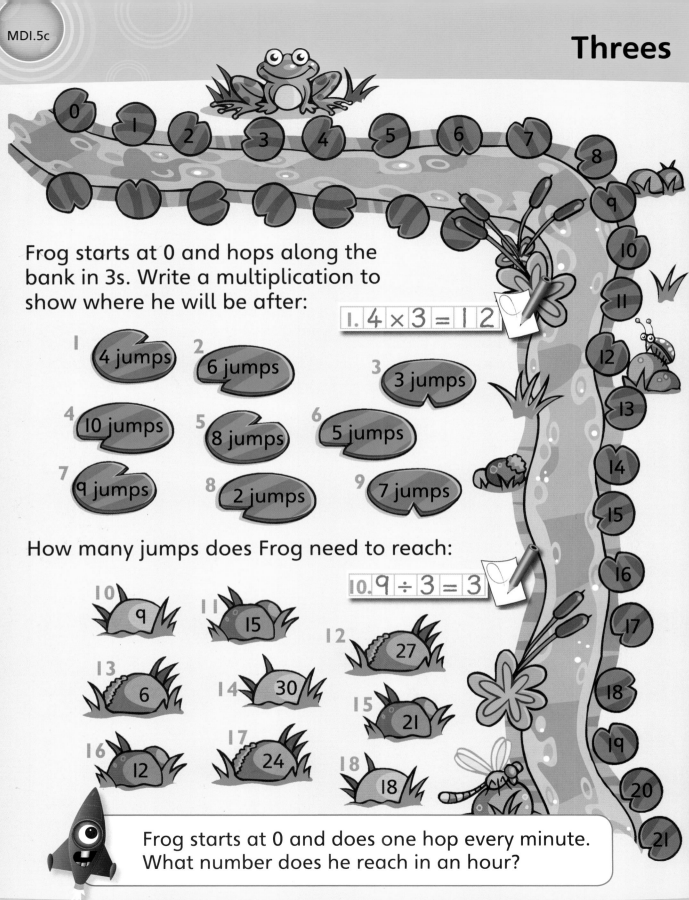

Frog starts at 0 and hops along the bank in 3s. Write a multiplication to show where he will be after:

1. $4 \times 3 = 12$

1 4 jumps
2 6 jumps
3 3 jumps
4 10 jumps
5 8 jumps
6 5 jumps
7 9 jumps
8 2 jumps
9 7 jumps

How many jumps does Frog need to reach:

10. $9 \div 3 = 3$

10 9
11 15
12 27
13 6
14 30
15 21
16 12
17 24
18 18

Frog starts at 0 and does one hop every minute. What number does he reach in an hour?

I can build up the 3 times-table

Threes and sixes

Each clover has three leaves. Write
the number of leaves in each set.

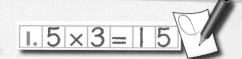

1

2

3

4

5

6

Copy and complete 10 rows. Write the last number in the:

1	2	3	4	5	6
7	8	9	10	11	

7. 2 4

7 4th row   8 7th row

9 2nd row   10 10th row

11 5th row   12 6th row

Write the next 10 row ends in the
pattern without drawing the table.

I can build up the 3 and 6 times-tables

Sixes

Write how many eggs in each set.

1. $3 \times 6 = 18$

1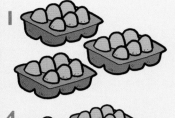

2

3

4

5

6

 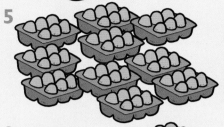 

7

8

9

 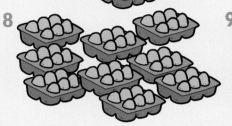 

 Which number of eggs between 40 and 50 will fit exactly in boxes of 6?

Write how many boxes can be filled with these eggs:

10. $18 \div 6 = 3$ boxes

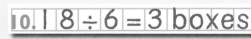

10

11

12

18 eggs

30 eggs

54 eggs

13

14

15

36 eggs

24 eggs

42 eggs

  I can build up the 6 times-table

Sixes

Write the position of the pointer
on each counting stick.

1.24

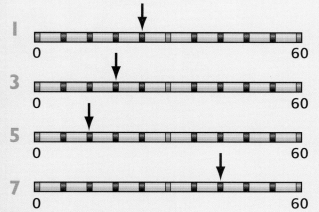

1
0   60

2
0   60

3
0   60

4
0   60

5
0   60

6
0   60

7
0   60

8
0   60

9 47 oranges are put into bags of six. How many bags
are there and how many oranges are left over?

10 Stickers are 6p each. Sanjay has a £1 coin,
and he buys one sticker every day for
a week. How much has he left?

11 Katie works in the corner shop on every day
except Sunday. How many days will Katie
have worked after 9 weeks?

Write your own word problem for this division: 24 ÷ 6 = 4.

Copy and complete.

12.36 ÷ 6 = 6

12 36 ÷ 6 = ☐   **13** 18 ÷ 6 = ☐   **14** 42 ÷ 6 = ☐

15 12 ÷ 6 = ☐   **16** 54 ÷ 6 = ☐   **17** 60 ÷ 6 = ☐

18 24 ÷ 6 = ☐   **19** 30 ÷ 6 = ☐   **20** 48 ÷ 6 = ☐

I can use the 6 times-table

1 Complete the 3s, then double to complete the 6s.

3s	3	6	9	12						
6s	6									

2 Complete the 1s and 5s, then add to complete the 6s.

1s	1	2	3	4						
5s	5	10								
6s	6									

3 Find the 6s by adding the 2s and 4s.

Find the 9s by adding the 3s and 6s.
How else could you have found the 9s?

Copy and complete.

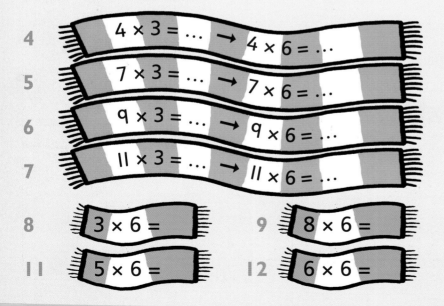

4 4 × 3 = ... → 4 × 6 = ...

5 7 × 3 = ... → 7 × 6 = ...

6 9 × 3 = ... → 9 × 6 = ...

7 11 × 3 = ... → 11 × 6 = ...

8 3 × 6 =

9 8 × 6 =

10 2 × 6 =

11 5 × 6 =

12 6 × 6 =

13 20 × 6 =

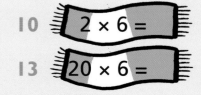

I can see patterns in times-tables

Multiplying and dividing

Write a division to match each set.

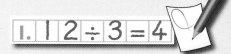

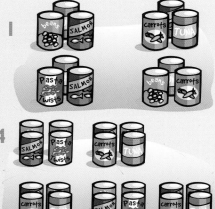

I

2

3

4

5

6

Write two multiplications for each.

Copy and complete. Write two divisions to match each.

7   3 × 5 =

8   4 × 6 =

9   5 × 7 =

10 2 × 8 =

11 6 × 3 =

12 10 × 4 =

13 8 × 5 =

14 5 × 4 =

15 9 × 10 =

Use these cards: 6   3   4   2   12   =   ÷   ×

Investigate how many different multiplications and divisions can be made.

12   ÷   4   =   3

I can make connections between multiplication and division problems

Multiplying and dividing

1 Copy and complete
the multiplication table.

×	1	2	3	4	5	6
1						
2				8		
3						
4						
5						
6						

2 Choose five numbers in the table,
and write two divisions for each.

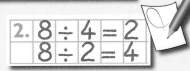

2. $8 \div 4 = 2$
$8 \div 2 = 4$

True or false?

3 Two 5p coins have the same
value as five 2p coins.

4 Five 10p coins have the same
value as ten 5p coins.

Use these
multiplication facts
to complete the sums:

$4 \times 12 = 48$ $6 \times 24 = 144$ $8 \times 15 = 120$

$8 \times 12 = 96$ $4 \times 24 = 96$

5 $48 \div 4 =$ ☐

6 $24 \times 6 =$ ☐

7 $120 \div 8 =$ ☐

8 $96 \div 4 =$ ☐

9 $96 \div 12 =$ ☐

10 $120 \div 15 =$ ☐

11 $15 \times 8 =$ ☐

12 $24 \times 4 =$ ☐

13 $144 \div 6 =$ ☐

I can make connections between multiplication and
division problems

Multiplying and dividing by 2

Write the cost of:

1.3 × 2p = 6p

1	3 throws	2	8 throws
3	4 throws	4	9 throws
5	6 throws	6	2 throws
7	10 throws	8	7 throws

9   17 throws

True or false?

10 If a number is multiplied by 2, the result is always an even number.

11 Half of 16 is the same as 16 ÷ 2.

12 If a number is divided by 2, the result is always an odd number.

13 If Karen paid 20p for six 2p stamps, how much change does she have?

14 There are 18 socks mixed up in a drawer. How many pairs will they make?

15 What is the difference between 8 times 2 and the number of 2s in 14?

16 What is the total of 7 multiplied by 2 and 20 divided by 2?

I can recall and use multiplication facts in the 2 times-table

Multiplying and dividing by 4

Write the position of each pointer on the stick.

1. 16

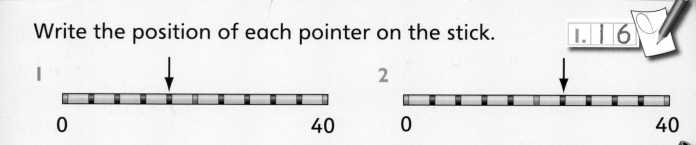

1   0   40

2   0   40

Copy and complete.

3. $12 \div 4 = 3$

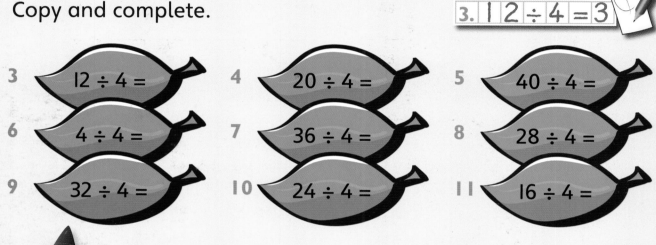

3   $12 \div 4 =$ 4 $20 \div 4 =$ 5 $40 \div 4 =$

6   $4 \div 4 =$ 7 $36 \div 4 =$ 8 $28 \div 4 =$

9   $32 \div 4 =$ 10 $24 \div 4 =$ 11 $16 \div 4 =$

Which numbers between 40 and 80 can be divided by 4?

12   How many season changes are there in 6 years?

13   Gary eats 4 slices of bread every day. How many slices does he eat in a fortnight?

14   The café has 4 chairs to each table. A coach party of 34 people come for a drink. How many tables will they need?

I can recall and use multiplication facts in the 4 times-table

Multiplying and dividing by 8

Write the position of each
pointer on the counting sticks.

1.40

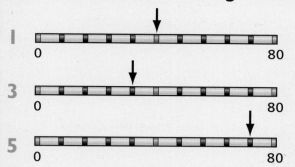

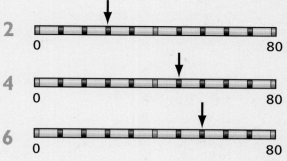

The children hold up one finger for each 8.
Write how many they have counted.

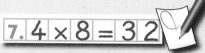
7. 4 × 8 = 32

 7

 10

 8

 11

 9

 12

How many fingers should the children hold up
to show multiples of 10? How many hands are
needed to show 240?

Copy and complete.

13. 2 × 8 = 16

13 2 × 8 = ☐	14 7 × 8 = ☐	15 5 × 8 = ☐
16 32 ÷ 8 = ☐	17 11 × 8 = ☐	18 64 ÷ 8 = ☐
19 6 × 8 = ☐	20 9 × 8 = ☐	21 0 × 8 = ☐
22 24 ÷ 8 = ☐	23 8 ÷ 8 = ☐	24 20 × 8 = ☐

 I can recall and use multiplication facts in the 8 times-table

Twos, fours and eights

Fill in the missing number
to make these balance.

$$4 \times 4 \quad = \quad 8 \times 2$$

1. $2 \times 4 = 8 \times 1$

1 $2 \times 4 = \boxed{} \times 1$ 2 $4 \times 6 = 8 \times \boxed{}$

3 $\boxed{} \times 2 = 4 \times 5$ 4 $32 \div \boxed{} = 2 \times 4$

5 $16 \div 2 = 2 \times \boxed{}$ 6 $36 \div 9 = \boxed{} \div 5$

Make up some balance questions, using
your 2, 4 and 8 facts, for a friend to solve.

7 Two sweets cost 18p. How much does one sweet cost?

8 Angus buys 4 pencils. The pencils cost 9p each. How much
   will this cost? How much change will he get from 40p?

The rugby competition has 2 leagues. Each league has 5 teams.

9 How many teams are there altogether?
10 A mini rugby team has 8 players. How many players
   are at the competition?
11 The top team in each league win medals. How many
   medals are needed altogether?

12 $2 \times 4 = \mathbf{8}$, $4 \times 2 = \mathbf{8}$, $8 \times 1 = \mathbf{8}$
   What other similar patterns can you find in the 2, 4 and
   8 times tables?

     I can multiply by 2, 4 and 8

Fives and tens

Copy and complete these divisions.

1. $35 \div 5 = 7$

1   $35 \div 5 =$ ☐   2 $80 \div 10 =$ ☐   3 $40 \div 5 =$ ☐

4   $60 \div 10 =$ ☐   5 $25 \div 5 =$ ☐   6 $70 \div 10 =$ ☐

7   $15 \div 5 =$ ☐   8 $40 \div 10 =$ ☐   9 $45 \div 5 =$ ☐

Write a matching multiplication for each.

10   Gill collects 5p coins in a jar. She collects 7 in the first week and 5 in the next week. How many coins does she now need to make £1?

11   45 players arrive for the school 5-a-side competition. How many teams can be made?

12   42 children are going by car on a school trip. Each car can take 5 children. How many cars are needed?

A clever way to divide by 5 is:

divide by 10, then double it

For example: $80 \div 5$ ⟶ $80 \div 10 = 8$

double 8 = 16

Use this clever way to try these:

13 $60 \div 5 =$ ☐   14 $90 \div 5 =$ ☐   15 $70 \div 5 =$ ☐

16 $160 \div 5 =$ ☐   17 $120 \div 5 =$ ☐   18 $230 \div 5 =$ ☐

I can recall and use division facts in the 5 and 10 times-tables

Fives and tens

Fill in the missing numbers
to make these balance.

$$5 \times 2 \quad = \quad 10 \times 1$$

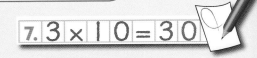

1.5 × 8 = 4 × 10

1 $5 \times 8 = \boxed{} \times 10$ 2 $5 \times 4 = 2 \times \boxed{}$

3 $6 \times \boxed{} = 3 \times \boxed{}$ 4 $50 \div \boxed{} = 5 \times 1$

5 $40 \div 5 = \boxed{} \div 10$ 6 $60 \div 5 = \boxed{} \div \boxed{}$

Make up some balance questions, using
your 5 and 10 facts, for a friend to solve.

How many all together?

7. 3 × 10 = 30

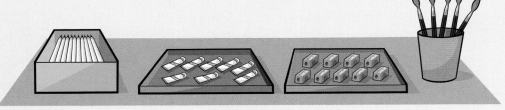

7   3 boxes of pencils   8   5 pots of paint brushes

9   5 glue trays   10 10 trays of pencil sharpeners

11 8 boxes of pencils   12 7 pots of paint brushes

13 10 glue trays   14 5 trays of pencil sharpeners

15 4 boxes of pencils   16 4 pots of paint brushes

17 $10 \times 4 = 40$. Half of **10** is **5**. Double **4** is **8**. So $5 \times 8 = 40$.
   Does this halving and doubling always work?

   I can multiply by 5 and 10

Threes and sixes

Copy and complete.

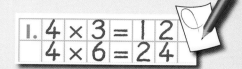

1. $4 \times 3 = 12$
$4 \times 6 = 24$

1	2	3	4	5
 4×3 4×6	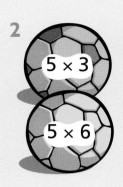 5×3 5×6	 8×3 8×6	 6×3 6×6	 9×3 9×6

Write the position of the pointer on each stick.

6. | 1 | 8 |

6
0   60

7
0   60

8
0   60

9
0   60

Football teams get 3 points for
a win and I point for a draw.
Write the number of points.

10. $6 \times 3 = 18$
$4 \times 1 = 4$
$18 + 4 = 22$ points

10 Ayr
6 wins
4 draws

11 Dundee
8 wins
3 draws

12 Inverness Caledonian
9 wins
5 draws

13 Partick Thistle
4 wins
6 draws

14 Ross County
7 wins
4 draws

15 Queen of the South
3 wins
2 draws

Find the points if teams get 4 points for a win
and 2 points for a draw

I can recall multiplication and division facts in the 3 and 6
times-table

29

Write out the 9 times-table. Use it to help you complete these.

1 $\boxed{} \times 9 = 18$ 2 $3 \times 9 = \boxed{}$ 3 $72 \div 9 = \boxed{}$

4 $\boxed{} \div 9 = 10$ 5 $4 \times 9 = \boxed{}$ 6 $9 \times \boxed{} = 9$

7 $\boxed{} \div 9 = 9$ 8 $\boxed{} \div 5 = 9$ 9 $\boxed{} \times 9 = 72$

10 $54 \div \boxed{} = 9$ 11 $\boxed{} \times 9 = 63$ 12 $36 \div \boxed{} = 9$

True or false?

13 In a multiplication fact where one number is 9, the answer has digits that add up to 9.

14 Three nines is an even number.

15 When a number is multiplied by 9, the answer is always odd.

16 If an even number is multiplied by 9 the answer is always odd.

17 Seven nines is a number that ends in 9.

18 If an odd number is multiplied by 9 the answer is always even.

I can recall multiplication facts in the 9 times-table

Nines

Write the position of each pointer.

1
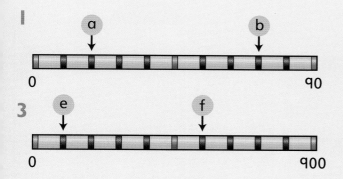

2
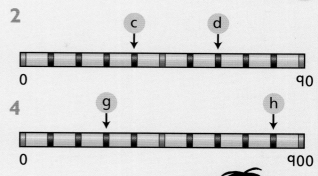

3

4

5   Pandit paid 9p for every sticker. He has 9 stickers.
    How much did he spend?

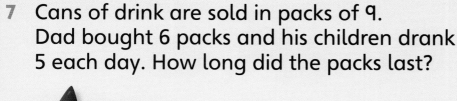

6   A dressmaker sewed 9 sequins onto
    each dress. She had 72 sequins. How
    many dresses did she decorate?

7   Cans of drink are sold in packs of 9.
    Dad bought 6 packs and his children drank
    5 each day. How long did the packs last?

Take a number, for example: 549
Add the digits: 5 + 4 + 9 = 18

Add the digits of the answer.
Keep going until you reach a single digit: 1 + 8 = 9

If the digit is 9, it means that
the number is in the ×9 table.

Write ten numbers greater than
500 that are in the ×9 table.

I can recall multiplication facts in the 9 times-table

Threes, sixes and nines

Fill in the missing number
to make these balance.

$$3 \times 3 \quad = \quad 9 \times 1$$

1 $3 \times 8 =$ ☐ $\times 4$ 2 $9 \times 2 = 6 \times$ ☐

1. $3 \times 8 = 6 \times 4$

3 $6 \times 2 = 3 \times$ ☐   4 $36 \div$ ☐ $= 2 \times 3$

5 $18 \div 2 = 3 \times$ ☐   6 $36 \div 9 =$ ☐ $\div 6$

Make up some balance questions, using
your 3, 6 and 9 facts, for a friend to solve.

How many all together?

7. $3 \times 7p = 21p$

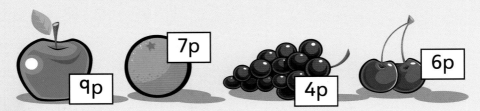

9p   7p   4p   6p

7 3 oranges   8 5 apples

9 6 bunches of grapes   10 3 lots of cherries

11 6 oranges   12 7 apples

13 9 bunches of grapes   14 7 lots of cherries

15 3 oranges   16 4 apples

17 3 bunches of grapes   18 9 lots of cherries

I can multiply by 3, 6 and 9

Multiplying by 10 and 100

Each hedgehog does a sponsored walk around their gardens. Write how far each walks after 10 laps of the garden.

1.450 m

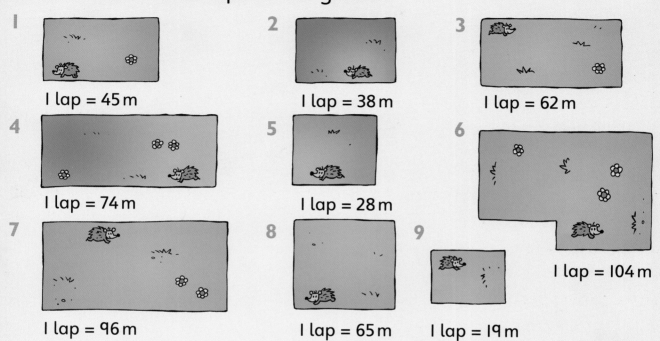

1 I lap = 45 m

2 I lap = 38 m

3 I lap = 62 m

4 I lap = 74 m

5 I lap = 28 m

6 I lap = 104 m

7 I lap = 96 m

8 I lap = 65 m

9 I lap = 19 m

Write how far after 100 laps of the garden.

One kilometre is 1000 metres. If the hedgehogs are sponsored £5 per kilometre, which ones earn more than £20 after 100 laps?

Copy and complete.

10. 35 × 10 = 350

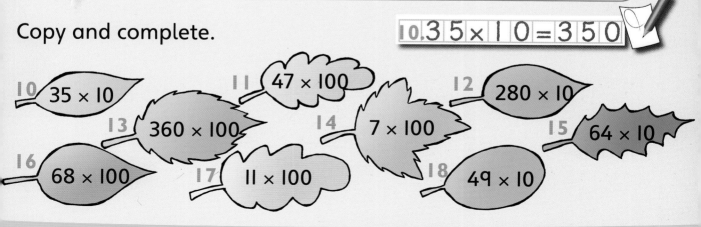

10 35 × 10

11 47 × 100

12 280 × 10

13 360 × 100

14 7 × 100

15 64 × 10

16 68 × 100

17 11 × 100

18 49 × 10

Multiplying by 10 and 100

These centipedes have 100 legs.
How many legs in each set?

1. $3 \times 100 = 300$

1

2

3

4

5

6

One minute is 60 seconds.
These centipedes can run 10
centimetres in 1 minute. How
far can they run in:

7. $8 \times 10 \, cm = 80 \, cm$

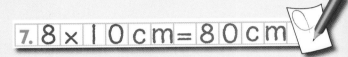

7 8 minutes	8 3 minutes	9 6 minutes
10 11 minutes	11 120 seconds	12 300 seconds

One hour is 60 minutes. How many centimetres
will a centipede run in 1 hour?

Copy and complete.

13. $4 \times 100 = 400$

13  $4 \times 100 =$

14  $7 \times 10 =$

15  $9 \times 100 =$

16  $6 \times 10 =$

17  $1 \times 100 =$

18  $2 \times 10 =$

 I can multiply by 10 and 100

Multiplying

The kangaroos hold a long jump competition. One metre is 100 centimetres. Write how many centimetres each kangaroo jumps.

1. $3 \times 100 \, cm = 300 \, cm$

1

3 metres

2

7 metres

3

5 metres

4

9 metres

5

6 metres

6

2 metres

 How many more metres would it take for each kangaroo to reach 10 m?

Write how many beads.

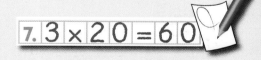

7. $3 \times 20 = 60$

7

8

9

10

11

12

 I want to make necklaces using 10 beads of each colour. How many necklaces can I make, and how many beads will be left over?

 I can multiply by multiples of 10 and by 100

Dividing by 10 and 100

Write the number of pounds by dividing by 10 or 100.

1. $4800 \div 100 = £48$

1
4800
1p coins

2
750
10p coins

3
6400
1p coins

4
800
1p coins

5
4600
10p coins

6
770
10p coins

7
690
10p coins

8
9800
10p coins

9
7400
1p coins

 Your aunt offers you either 10p a day for a year or £3 a month for a year. Which is better?

Copy and complete.

10. $840 \div 10 = 84$

10 $840 \div 10 =$ ☐   11 $5600 \div 100 =$ ☐   12 $7600 \div 10 =$ ☐

13 $7900 \div 100 =$ ☐   14 $4800 \div 100 =$ ☐   15 $8500 \div 100 =$ ☐

16 $950 \div 10 =$ ☐   17 $480 \div 10 =$ ☐   18 $8000 \div 10 =$ ☐

 I can divide by 10 and 100

Write the cost of the masks.

I. $3 \times 20p = 60p$

 20p

 40p

 30p

 50p

1   3 clown masks

2   2 teddy bear masks

3   5 alien masks

4   7 monkey masks

5   6 clown masks

6   4 teddy bear masks

7   3 alien masks

8   9 monkey masks

9   10 alien masks and 4 monkey masks

10   6 teddy bear masks and 5 clown masks

How many of each mask can you buy for £5?

Copy and complete.

II. $3 \times 30 = 90$

11    3×30

12    5×40

13   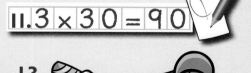 6×30

14   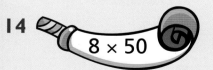 8×50

15    40×3

16    4×20

17    50×5

18   9×30

19   2×60

Multiplication facts

Write three more multiplication facts for each calculation.

$$1.\ 3 \times 6 = 18 \qquad 30 \times 6 = 180$$
$$3 \times 60 = 180 \qquad 30 \times 60 = 1800$$

1 $3 \times 6 =$ 2 $4 \times 8 =$ 3 $3 \times 7 =$ 4 $4 \times 5 =$

5 $5 \times 7 =$ 6 $4 \times 9 =$ 7 $6 \times 5 =$ 8 $6 \times 9 =$

9 $3 \times 4 =$ 10 $8 \times 4 =$ 11 $8 \times 7 =$ 12 $8 \times 9 =$

How many multiplication calculations can you find that have the answer 240?

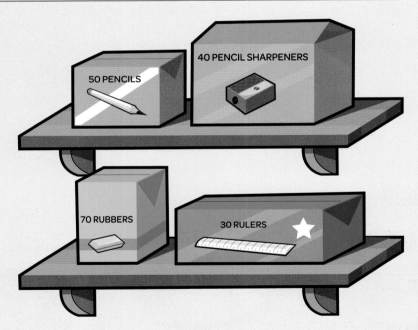

50 PENCILS

40 PENCIL SHARPENERS

70 RUBBERS

30 RULERS

13 How many pencils in 40 boxes?

14 How many rubbers in 20 boxes?

15 How many rulers in 80 boxes?

16 How many pencil sharpeners in 90 boxes?

I can use my knowledge of table facts and of multiplying by 10 to make new multiplication facts

Write two more multiplication facts for each calculation.

1. 5 × 6 = 30
500 × 6 = 3000   5 × 600 = 3000

1 5 × 6 =

2 5 × 8 =

3 5 × 7 =

4 4 × 4 =

5 4 × 7 =

6 4 × 9 =

7 6 × 5 =

8 6 × 7 =

9 6 × 9 =

10 9 × 5 =

11 9 × 4 =

12 9 × 9 =

How many multiplication calculations can you find that have the answer 2400? What about 4800? What patterns can you see?

13 Ella's mum is saving up for a car.
Each week she saves £40.
She saves for 50 weeks.
How much money has she saved?

14 A coal lorry has 70 bags of coal.
Each bag weighs 30 kg.
How many kg of coal are there?

15 Jamal is raising money for charity.
His target is £4800. Does he need to raise
£40 a week for 20 weeks,
£50 a week for 30 weeks
or £80 a week for 60 weeks?

To Charity

from Jamal   £4800

I can use my knowledge of table facts and of multiplying by 100 to make new multiplication facts

Multiplying

Copy and complete.

$$1. \ 33 \times 4 = 132$$

1 $33 \times 4 = \boxed{}$ 2 $32 \times 5 = \boxed{}$ 3 $21 \times 9 = \boxed{}$

4 $64 \times 5 = \boxed{}$ 5 $47 \times 2 = \boxed{}$ 6 $13 \times 5 = \boxed{}$

7 $48 \times 9 = \boxed{}$ 8 $21 \times 4 = \boxed{}$ 9 $15 \times 4 = \boxed{}$

10 $73 \times 4 = \boxed{}$ 11 $40 \times 9 = \boxed{}$ 12 $27 \times 9 = \boxed{}$

13 Biscuits cost 17p.
How much change will
you have from £1 if
you buy 5 biscuits?

14 Kevin the
kangaroo travels
6 m with every hop.
How far will he have
gone after 25 hops?

15 Raffle tickets cost 30p each.
A book of 5 tickets costs
£1·35. How much do you
save by buying the book?

16 3 times a number is half of
5×6. What is the number?

$\boxed{} \times \boxed{} \times \boxed{} = 24.$ What could the three numbers
be? (Two might be the same.)

I can multiply a 2-digit number by a 1-digit number

Doubling

Multiply these numbers by 2, by splitting them into tens and units.

```
1. 2 × 10 = 20   2 × 3 = 6   20 + 6 = 26
   2 × 13 = 26
```

1 13	2 24	3 31	4 42
5 51	6 47	7 18	8 36
9 54	10 58	11 68	12 78

What is 2 × 75?
Use this to calculate 4 × 75 and 8 × 75.
What about 16 × 75?

13   A bag of apples costs 78p.
How much change will you get from
£2 if you buy 2 bags of apples?

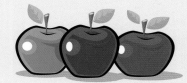

14   Cameron is cooking an omelette. The recipe
asks for 54 g of butter and 67 g of cheese.
He doubles the recipe. How much butter
and cheese should he use?

15   An MP3 player is on sale at
half price for £57. How much
would it normally cost?

I can use my table facts to work out multiplication calculations

1   Naresh collects 10p coins.
He has saved £7·80.
How many coins is this?

2   Sally gets £5 pocket money
every week. There are 52 weeks
in a year. How much does this
cost her parents every year?

Invent a rule for these, starting by multiplying by
10 and 100:

3   Multiplying by 50   4   Multiplying by 200

5   Multiplying by 11   6   Multiplying by 9

Try the rules on these numbers:

43   18   160

Copy and complete.

7. $73 \times 10 = 730$

7   $73 \times 10 =$ ☐   8 $42 \times 100 =$ ☐

9   $39 \times 100 =$ ☐   10 $860 \times 10 =$ ☐

11 $47 \times 5 =$ ☐   12 $96 \times 20 =$ ☐

13 $28 \times 50 =$ ☐   14 $86 \times 20 =$ ☐

15 $32 \times 200 =$ ☐   16 $38 \times 50 =$ ☐

I can use my table facts to multiply by multiples of 10 and 100

Dividing

Write two divisions to match each set of tiles.

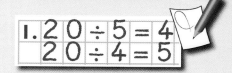

1. $20 \div 5 = 4$
2. $20 \div 4 = 5$

1 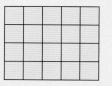 2 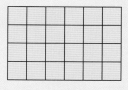 3 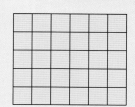 4

5 6

Draw some sets of tiles from which only one division can be written.

Class 4 has 27 children, who need to be split into teams. Write how many teams can be made, and how many children are left over.

7. $27 \div 3 = 9$ teams exactly

7
teams of 3

8
teams of 4

9
teams of 2

10
teams of 10

11
teams of 5

12
teams of 6

Find different ways of splitting 24 children into teams of equal size, with no children left over.

I can use table facts to help me work out division calculations

MDI.10

Dividing

Use each list to help you complete these divisions with remainders.

$$1. \; 15 \div 4 = 3 \, r \, 3$$

| 4 | 8 | 12 | 16 | 20 | 24 | 28 | 32 | 36 | 40 |

1 15 ÷ 4 =   **2** 29 ÷ 4 =   **3** 38 ÷ 4 =   **4** 22 ÷ 4 =

| 5 | 10 | 15 | 20 | 25 | 30 | 35 | 40 | 45 | 50 |

5 23 ÷ 5 =   **6** 18 ÷ 5 =   **7** 44 ÷ 5 =   **8** 36 ÷ 5 =

The list for 4s and the list for 5s have two numbers in common: 20 and 40. Find some other pairs of lists that have numbers in common.

How many chair lifts are needed for:

$$9. \; 13 \div 3 = 4 \, r \, 1$$
$$5 \; chairs$$

9 13 people   **10** 22 people   **11** 28 people

How many cable cars are needed for:

12 21 people   **13** 43 people   **14** 82 people

How many toboggans are needed for:

15 17 people   **16** 28 people   **17** 61 people

Chair lifts 3 people only

Cable cars 4 people only

Toboggans 5 people only

What number of people can fit exactly into chair lifts, into cable cars and into toboggans?

I can answer division questions with remainders

Dividing

True or false?

1 $18 \div 4 = 4 \text{ r } 2$

2 $21 \div 5 = 4 \text{ r } 1$

3 $36 \div 10 = 6 \text{ r } 3$

4 $25 \div 3 = 8 \text{ r } 2$

5 $23 \div 2 = 11 \text{ r } 1$

6 $38 \div 4 = 8 \text{ r } 2$

7 $26 \div 3 = 8 \text{ r } 2$

8 $43 \div 5 = 9 \text{ r } 3$

9 $25 \div 4 = 6 \text{ r } 1$

Rewrite the false ones with the correct answer.

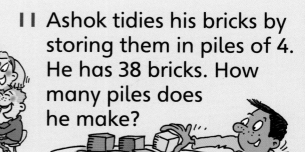

10 Five friends go for a burger. The bill comes to £16. If each person paid with £5, how much change would they each receive?

11 Ashok tidies his bricks by storing them in piles of 4. He has 38 bricks. How many piles does he make?

12 Jenny eats 4 slices of toast every day. A loaf has 17 slices. How many days will they last?

13 Mel is saving to buy 5p stickers. She has enough money to buy 7 stickers and have 3p left over. How much has she saved?

7 gives a remainder of 1 when divided by both 2 and 3.
$7 \div 2 = 3 \text{ r } 1$ $7 \div 3 = 2 \text{ r } 1$

Find other numbers that also give a remainder of 1 when divided by both 2 and 3.

Find numbers that give a remainder of 1 when divided by both 2 and 5.

I can answer division questions with remainders

Dividing by 5 is the same as working out how many 5s are in a number.
I can work out how many 5s are in a number by thinking about how many 10s are in it and doubling this.

87 has eight 10s but it has a remainder of 7 which can make another group of 5 with 2 left over. 87 is seventeen 5s remainder 2.

Number	How many 10s?	How many 5s?	Another group?	Answer
87	8 r 7	16 r 7	yes	17 r 2

Divide these by 5

$1. 89 \div 5 = 17 r 4$

1 89   2 76   3 54   4 66

5 94   6 99   7 102   8 127

Write a different calculation to check each of your division answers.

9 If Donald shares his sweets between 5 people, there are 3 sweets left over. If he shares them between 2 people, there is 1 sweet left over. If he shares them between 4 people, there are 3 sweets left over. Donald has more than 50 sweets. How many could he have?

Multiplying

1 Ian bought 4 apples at 23p each and 3 oranges at 32p each. How much change did he have from £5?

2 The bus fare to work is 24p each way. What is the cost for a 5-day week? How much cheaper is a travel pass, costing £1·85 a week?

3 Tickets for the match cost £34 for adults and £18 for children. What is the cost for a family of 4 adults and 3 children?

Change the numbers in the questions to make them very easy to solve.

Find how to arrange the digits like this: ☐ × ☐☐
to make these answers.

4 3 4 5 ⟶ 215

5 6 2 7 ⟶ 182

6 4 8 6 ⟶ 288

7 5 2 8 ⟶ 140

Use number cards 0–9.
Choose three to make a multiplication like this:

☐☐ × ☐

Using the cards, write down five easy calculations and five hard calculations. Choose one from each group and explain why they are easy or hard.

I can multiply 2-digit numbers by 1-digit numbers

Tennis racket £64

Swimming costume £36

Rugby shirt £37

Trainers £42

Write the cost. Before you start, explain how you will find each answer.

1 6 rugby shirts

2 8 tennis rackets

3 2 pairs of trainers

4 3 swimming costumes

Solve these questions. Explain how you will find each answer.

5 Eva buys 9 tennis balls. She spends £36. How much does one tennis ball cost?

6 Jake, Rohan and Ayesha want to buy a treadmill at £126. How much money must they each give?

7 6 friends share 86 ping pong balls between them. How many ping pong balls do they each get and how many are left over?

Write three different multiplying or dividing word problems so that:
- Your partner can answer the first question without any working out.
- Your partner can solve the second question mentally, writing notes to help them.
- Your partner needs to write out the answer to the third question in full.

I can use different ways to solve multiplication and division questions and explain why I chose the method